The Keys Of Awareness

The Book Of Wonder

The Keys Of Awareness
The Book Of Wonder

From a series of original paintings by
RACHAEL WILMOT

Published by Illustrious Artworks
ISBN 978-0-9557363-1-5

www.illustriousartworks.com

Contents

Each Key is a world in itself

The Keys Of Awareness
The Book Of Wonder

Preface

I've always known about 'the wonder', and working as a healer I have been able to place this in context, and become aware of the flow of energy that controls and influences our existence. The Keys of Awareness are an attempt to show others these 'intangible energies' and 'the wonder'.

In recent years I have become aware of many past lives I've had, from caveman times before language, medieval life in Scotland, a slave life, a short life in The First World War, to life in the 1920's and 1930's. I've understood and seen, through these past lives, the continuity of existence through the resolution of problems over many lives. Through all of these there is the pull of karmic energy which puts the Human Condition into perspective. This theme has continued into the painting of The Keys.

The Keys of Awareness are the access to intangible worlds through energy forms, colour, space, and light, that connect you to their story and timeless quality. When you move deeper into the Key you tune into its' 'frequency' and harmony through your sensitivity, openness, and contemplation. Spiritual evolution comes through this expansion, like the rays of the sun radiating and influencing, while your thoughts and intellectual discovery go through other stages of development and achievement.

This journey takes you from the tangible qualities of colour and form into intangible and spiritual states of being. Using The Keys, you can change and expand your evolutionary state of awareness.

Rachael Wilmot

*"The intangible exists, unseen,
in that which is here."*

Introduction

If you look at the Earth from space you will see its' colour and atmosphere, and the sea and land masses. As you move closer and enter the atmosphere you'll see rocks and trees, water, and changes in the landscape. Moving closer still, you'll see the tremendous movement in the people, the animals, the weather, and all the elemental qualities of the planet. On a deeper level again you might become aware of the evolution of the Earth.

In the same way, as you look at a person, there is the physical and material presence, and just below the surface, the emotions and personality. Deeper still, you pass through thoughts, notions and ideas, the imagination, and levels of awareness. On the deepest level is the evolution of understanding.

The world isn't just a physical and material place. No two chairs, two rooms, two people, or two days, are the same, even though physically they may appear, at first glance, to be alike. Each person, each thing, each situation, and every element in the world, moves through, and rests in, an intangible energy. We are surrounded by intangible energies, like fish in water, or the birds in the air. The intangible energies are produced all the time, by people, plants, things, and the weather, and even the spaces themselves. The intangible energies define, and alter, your state of being. The intangible energies influence and bring about change in the physical world, and will affect the way you feel and think.

> *"Physically alive in a place, that is itself alive.*
> *Moving through in three dimensions."*

You gain more energy and vitality from being aware of these intangible energies, and use them to increase your confidence and enjoyment of being alive here. You experience and work with these intangible energies all the time, and you have done so all your life, but possibly have not recognised it. These intangible energies are seen through listening, understanding, and accepting. You may be accustomed to living through your thoughts, emotions, and physical sensations, but there is another more spontaneous way of seeing the world. Realising, recognising, and seeing, these intangible energies for yourself, is the key. The Keys of Awareness are about looking directly and seeing "the intangible."

Each person follows their own pattern of thinking, which defines their awareness. Stepping out of this pattern leads to Direct Awareness. Direct Awareness happens when you leave behind your experiences, opinions and views, and allow yourself to open-up to the world.

In order to experience these intangible energies, you need to take a small step. For a moment, forget about yourself and your concerns, your opinions, and your abilities. There is something else besides yourself. You only have to be open "to what is possible". It is you, not some mysterious technique or force, that is the link to the intangible. You are the link. This link, or Direct Awareness, is available to you all the time. "Seeing what is" is the wonder.

It is not possible to fully understand or appreciate The Keys inwardly through thought. When you think, you move into your own mind and its internal machinations. Understanding can only come through a perception of The Keys through Direct Awareness. It's not about 'dealing with the world', but 'what you do' without being drawn into thoughts and considerations, complications and involvements. It is by *not* exercising control over your thoughts or experiences that you become open to perceive the truth. Your thoughts, feelings, and beliefs, are only a part or aspect of you, even though they can dominate your life.

Beyond physical appearances there is an energy which you can 'see', know, and feel. It is like looking with, or through, a sensitivity, rather than depending on appearances and opinions. An awareness of, or an openness to, this flow of energy brings the intangible to life. This is the beginning of 'Direct Awareness'. By being receptive you are open to a new dimension of awareness, and you can only do this by letting go of thought, and any view you place on things. Beyond what you think you see, there is an energy and vitality waiting to be discovered.

For example, when you go out for a walk, you might choose a familiar route or simply see it as an exercise, and enjoy the activity. You could also notice other things, like the weather, time of day, or season, the sights, sounds, colours and smells, and the atmosphere. As you walk through the whole scene you become Directly Aware of the situation you are in. The whole of you enters into a relationship with the situation, and the world is revealed to you. As you look, your awareness occupies the same space as each thing you look at. You then begin to feel the energy that is outside you as it truly is. You are aware of things as they are, without your activities or opinion. Everything in the world will talk to you, *if you let it*, and it will do so through colour, form, energy and flow. The whole of the physical world is charged with intangible energies which illuminate and enliven everything. You just need to be open enough to see all of this.

The Flow of Energy

You look with your eyes, and you listen with your ears, but you also feel information and sensations. Certain sounds, sights, colours, movements, and fragrances, also affect the way you take in information and understand the world. There is a two-way exchange of energy. Energy comes in through your senses, but this is filtered through your perception, which relies on your experience, your mind, and your habits. How you feel about things, your way of seeing, and your attitude and response, pushes your energy out, and affects, dilutes or diverts, the nature of the energy coming in. There is an almost automatic response on an energy level which reinforces, or asserts, your opinion and attitude. To step out of this automatic response and reaction you need to become directly aware of the energy, and specifically colour, without opinion or preference.

Colour reflects the physical, emotional, mental, and spiritual, aspects of your life. This energy response, through colour, is quicker than thought. Your energy field, and your own thoughts and feelings, can actually be seen in full colour, and colour is one of the ways that you can tune-in to this energy. In this way, seeing and using colour makes working with the energies easy. You can represent the energy spectrum through colour, so that the full range of colours are the intangible energies seen physically. Each colour is a different state of being. *It is not the meaning of each colour, but the immediate reception of its energy,* that is the key, beyond your thoughts and experience.

Seeing colour *as energy* is the key. There is no worldly context or intellectual label to this, because this is being directly receptive to energy, not through thought or idea, but as Direct Awareness. An awareness of, or an openness to, this flow of energy, represented by colour, is the beginning of 'Direct Awareness'. Colour provides you with energy and information, and the more you understand your response to colour, the fuller your life becomes through *a direct awareness of the energy in colour.*

There is a flow of energy that governs everything. The direction of the flow can go inwards towards mental speculation and concerns, or outwards to a relaxation of thought that opens you to another source of information and vitality. In this flow there needs to be a balance, much like the natural rhythm of the breath in and out, or waves breaking on the shore, expanding, and returning to the sea, or the regular beat of the wings of a bird in flight. The amount of energy coming in or going out has a profound effect on your awareness.

If you were to follow the flow of this 'mental' energy from the deep pull inwards, to a lighter expanding, letting go, you would see the nature and weight of this energy. Materialistic, reactive, and involved, thoughts are heavy, and the energy of these inner thoughts is of a slower nature, even though your worldly involvements may not appear to you as slow or heavy. Lighter thoughts are introduced as enthusiasm in a quicker speed of energy through acceptance and openness. Ideas and creative thoughts use this lighter energy to make changes and improvements in your life. Your imagination gives you extra information, which adds another dimension. Lighter and quicker still is intuition, apparently not grounded in reality, where anything is possible. This is the 'open realm' beyond your own inner thoughts and feelings.

In this 'open realm' intuition has a life of its own. Inspiration now appears as a sudden realisation out of nowhere. This positive energy comes directly from the intangible realms with a quicker and greater impact, and can influence any area of your life cutting through heavier thoughts. It is possible to live within this inspired state, open to 'the wonder' of everything, The Keys give you access to the open realm.

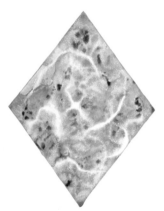

"Light is forming,
but it is already light."

The Keys Of Awareness

The Keys are the visible balance of intangible energies. It is as if colour is placed under a microscope, and you can see it moving and teeming with life. This is the energy in colour. Within each type of energy there are subtle changes in colour, which produce certain effects, insights and expressions. The Keys show the intangible energies through colour, scale, space, shape and flow, and have an elemental power that cannot be expressed in words, or through thought, or concepts.

Each Key, much like a musical key, represents a balance, mood, or harmony, of a number of notes, or energies, that produce an effect. Natural elements, light, air, and snow, etc., all show the movement of the intangible energies. The light, for instance, is a spontaneous positive expression, that it's possible to create from within. These are all aspects of your inner and outer self. By looking at The Keys you can tune-in to your own energies, and the intangible energies around you. Each Key has a 'frequency' that you tune into to energise you, or impart trust or assurance. As when you look at a painting, or listen to music, you move outwards towards a dialogue, or relationship, as you seek to discover more.

The Keys introduce you to other intangible states of being which can be seen as separate intangible worlds. These are places of wonder and spiritual understanding. Each Key is a world with its own atmosphere, and its own energy and dynamic. Each Key is alive, and you will move into the living realms and dimensions of each place. You inhabit these worlds as they relate to your worldly and spiritual awareness, and your mental and physical well-being. As you look at The Key with Direct Awareness you naturally align your own energy to the energy of The Key. Each Key represents a different state of awareness and a perfect state of understanding, giving emotional security, certainty, and confidence.

The keys also have a symbolic scenario. The scenario bridges the gap between pure spiritual energies and your life experience through repeated karmic patterns, the human condition, and your emotional life and connections. These are like stories or legends passed down through time. The text is there to reveal other connections for you to consider on another level of understanding. It is for you to enter The Keys, and the text provides a clue to these profound states.

The Keys are also grouped in sections, to show you the evolution of your expanding awareness, and the further potential open to you. Each section deals with a topic of existence, awareness, or understanding, and each Key within a section develops the theme.

Each Key is geometrically shaped. This shape adds a particular strength and focus. It connects the intangible energies to your intuitive mental intent, anchoring the fluidity and colour within a stable boundary. The shape of The Key establishes a 'strength of space' or focus of power or intention. These shapes fulfil basic needs of your character and well-being, and when you occupy these spaces you take on these qualities.

*"You illuminate this world,
and create a place in the infinite."*

Strength of Space

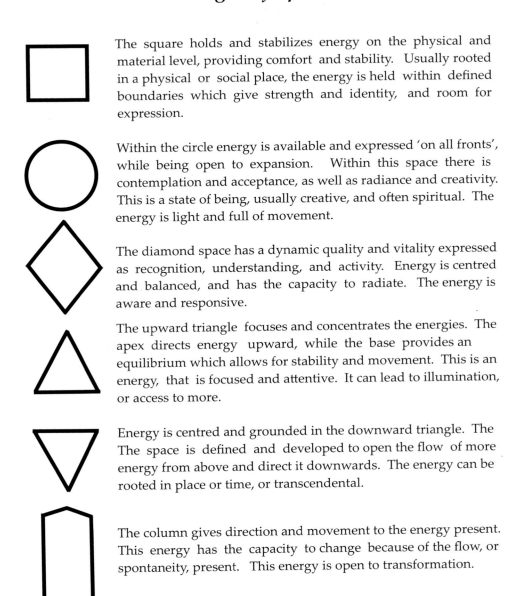

The square holds and stabilizes energy on the physical and material level, providing comfort and stability. Usually rooted in a physical or social place, the energy is held within defined boundaries which give strength and identity, and room for expression.

Within the circle energy is available and expressed 'on all fronts', while being open to expansion. Within this space there is contemplation and acceptance, as well as radiance and creativity. This is a state of being, usually creative, and often spiritual. The energy is light and full of movement.

The diamond space has a dynamic quality and vitality expressed as recognition, understanding, and activity. Energy is centred and balanced, and has the capacity to radiate. The energy is aware and responsive.

The upward triangle focuses and concentrates the energies. The apex directs energy upward, while the base provides an equilibrium which allows for stability and movement. This is an energy, that is focused and attentive. It can lead to illumination, or access to more.

Energy is centred and grounded in the downward triangle. The The space is defined and developed to open the flow of more energy from above and direct it downwards. The energy can be rooted in place or time, or transcendental.

The column gives direction and movement to the energy present. This energy has the capacity to change because of the flow, or spontaneity, present. This energy is open to transformation.

*"Fire from Heaven brings
inspiration down to Earth"*

How to use the Keys
Through Direct Awareness

We all have opinions and notions and feelings, but here you'll need to put them to one side for a moment. Opinions don't really leave much room for anything else, and your feelings will only confirm, or enclose, what you already know. Putting your opinion and notions to one side for a moment, leaves you open to something else. There is more to the world than your experience and opinions, and as your awareness grows you will have the capacity to go much further, and see more. Each Key is a level of understanding, and a way to perceive, the intangible energies.

Lots of positive changes will take place as you respond to the energies of The Keys. This way of looking, through Direct Awareness (with an open sensitivity without thought) creates awareness, allowing you to take-in more energy, or release energy that has become fixed. The Keys open your awareness to dimensionless space. They allow freedom from thought and communicate a different state of influence and stability. Holding and looking at The Key is a way to recharge, balance, and gain contact with, profound states of awareness. Each Key imparts positive energy.

Each aspect of the human condition is answered by The Keys. There are 'universal' issues of existence, awareness, security, and identity, which you may personalise into a problem. If so, you can select a Key you are drawn to (all The Keys are set-out on the back pages), or go to the Contents pages and look through the section titles for an appropriate theme to answer your question or resolve an issue. Look through the section to find The Key that is closest to your enquiery.

SELECT A KEY that you are drawn to, sit quietly, and let it reveal the subtlety of itself. You can select any Key on your feeling, sensitivity, or instinctive preference. This takes you away from that part of the mind that deals with reason and logic, or with standards and opinions. The text explains what the energy does, but The Key is brought into action only when you look at it through Direct Awareness.

Each colour has an energy that you can become aware of as you look at it. Through colour you enter into another world of energy, and as this begins to happen the colours may seem to move, or feel comforting or nourishing, calming or energising. You may feel drawn to certain areas and want to move into them, or follow them, or areas seem to move out towards you. Some areas may feel warm, or cool and spacious. The scale will change and you will be drawn into the scene. In The Keys it isn't possible to know the scale of what you are looking at because there are no familiar reference points or worldly comparisons. You will make the discovery that awareness has no dimensions. The Keys may seem huge and expansive as you move through them, or quiet and calming. Through your awareness, your energy responds and changes with The Key. There is a sense of weight and lightness, movement and speed, light and colour, within The Keys *which you take in as pure energy*, not as thought. The Keys provide an avenue of awareness, through which all these different states can be revealed.

Selecting any of The Keys is a very personal choice, and The Keys you choose will be right for you. The Keys will inform, guide, or reflect, your expanding awareness. When you choose a Key look at the others in the same section for a deeper insight into your situation. Choices are made spontaneously on the feeling of what is right for you, without qualification or justification. Direct Awareness is the key, and The Keys unlock the potential. The Keys of Awareness will introduce you to other subtle realms that are endless and ever changing.

You are part of the physical and the intangible, and this is the 'wonder' which you can see everyday, not only within The Keys. This leads to the state of living everyday in 'Direct Awareness', away from the rigours of the mind. The world is a 'wonder'. Here and now in the present moment is the meeting place of the tangible and intangible, and you are at the centre of it all.

" I am physical, and stand within the intangible. "

The Energy Forms

In each Key the intangible energies are seen as energy forms.

These energy forms and flows represent different expressions of energy. Each Key brings a structure to the individual energy forms, which are like musical notes, expressed in a particular key imparting a certain understanding and awareness. Each Key is a perfect balance of energy and form, that gives permanence and security. Here are the energy forms that are found in The Keys. These are the energies that move our thoughts and feelings. They are not the thoughts and feelings themselves but the energies behind them.

Continuous Energy

This spinning energy creates a glassy surface refracting curves of light outward. This stops thoughts going inward, keeping you in the present. There is a vitality and clarity to this energy that gives direction and purpose.

'The Untarnished Shield'

Directional Dynamic Energy

A fast flowing energy that reflects light. This energy over-runs underlying forms, but is still influenced by them to produce new effects and images. This energy is refreshing and cool, and wakes you up into action, allowing choices to be made, and intentions expressed.

'Behind the Veil'

14

Crystal Energy

The movement and concentration of energy creates an almost physical form. Sensitivity is receptive and focused. This provides clarity and information.

'The Guiding Star'

Sand Energy

An energy that covers through time, like moving sand. This energy has a weight, and comfort, that shifts and changes slowly. This energy is slow moving, causing you to slow down, and go at your own speed, unhurried, without any pressure from outside influences. You can let events unfold in their own time. This is a settled energy bringing in security and assurance.

'The Present Moment'

15

Cloud Energy

Energy can be seen as clouds, cushioning and bridging one state to another. They cushion change. These clouds, or energy forms, can be so thick as to obscure your view. The clouds can also cushion us from too much information and act as a filter for our thoughts and emotions. Much like the clouds protect us from the intensity of the sun, so these energy forms filter the light of awareness from the intensity and purity of the intangible realms. We could not stand too much profound awareness in our day to day lives, so we need to filter this energy to provide the right amount of nourishment. We can relax into this energy form and calm the concentration. Sometimes clouds disperse like morning mist over water as light and warmth break through, revealing the scene. Clouds separate and join different types of energy or awareness.

The Rainbow Golden Dawn'
'Forgiveness'
Shining Out'
'The Winged Dragon'
'The Guiding Star'

Interwoven Energy

Here the energy forms a pattern of connecting lines and spaces. Each separate area becomes part of the whole. Points of light provide identification and location. This energy provides protection, comfort, and connection.

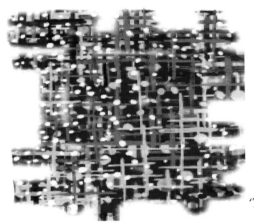

'Everlasting Flame'
'The Tapestry of Life'

Metallic Energy

The shiny surface concentrates light into a one dimensional field. This energy is so intense and concentrated, it will eventually lead to stress, unless it is modified by cloud energy.

'Living in the clouds'

17

Falling Snow Energy

This energy introduces gentle movement without sound. Being quiet allows a downward movement as a softening. This will have the effect of calming your emotions.

'Soundless Space'
'Kindness'
'Inner Light'

Tendril Energy

The Tendrils show the tactile freedom of movement. They partake in the flow, and are supported, moved and liberated, by the energy they rest in. They respond to the currents of energy. They are separate and free flowing in the surrounding energy and sing-out, creating light and positive energy, always receptive to the new. This is the freedom to act, and to respond in your own way. This energy form attracts more positive and vital free flowing energy, bringing freedom from restriction.

'The Seasons'
'Inner Light'
'Everlasting Flame'

Luminous and Translucent Energy

This energy glows and illuminates, and affects the surrounding energies with a sparkling clarity. Here, thought is illuminated and the mind opens to the depth and subtlety of things.
'Pillar of Flame'
'Testament'
'Kindness'
'The Crescent Array'
'Expansion'

Luminous and Translucent Energy

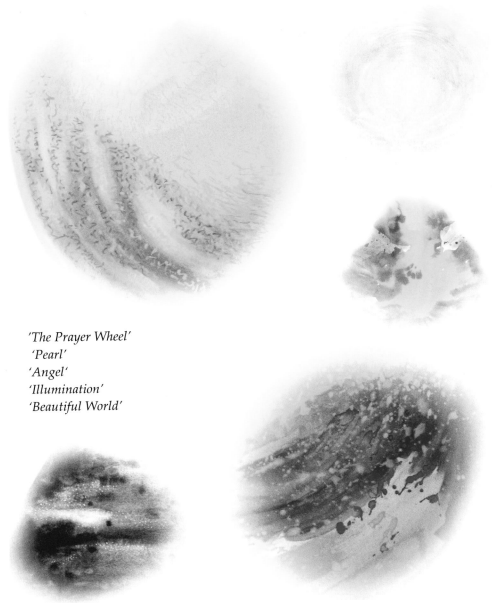

'The Prayer Wheel'
'Pearl'
'Angel'
'Illumination'
'Beautiful World'

Effervescent Energy

A spontaneous creative energy. The brightest white particles are dissolving, and breaking free. As they shoot off in all directions they get brighter, eventually producing areas of brilliant light. There is no direction to this energy as it expands spontaneously. This is the opposite of effort, and expressed as enthusiasm or spontaneous action without thought. This energy is vibrant and effervescent, making light. Literally making light of things. Forming stars by day.

'Contact'
'Inner Light'
'Kindness'
'Cornucopia'

Effervescent Energy

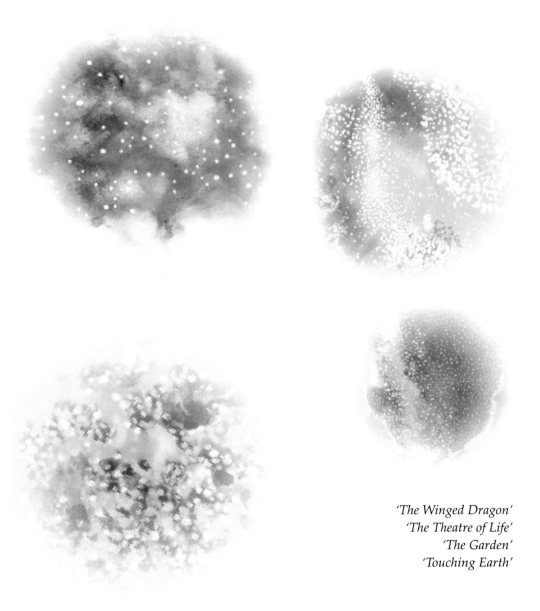

'The Winged Dragon'
'The Theatre of Life'
'The Garden'
'Touching Earth'

Flame Energy

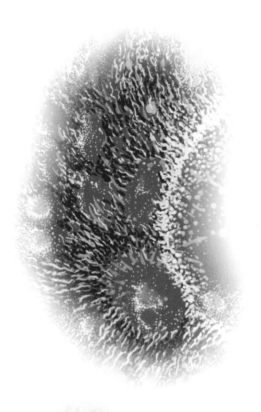

This energy is seen as flames of pure energy, without smoke or fuel. These are the flames of perception, which listen, see, and know. This is the perception, and awareness, of all the senses. Beyond the noise and machinations of the mental and emotional thought processes, there is the subtlety of perception. This takes place in a vast profound silence, which is full of life and activity. Shimmering embers of light energy create a wind, flickering the flames of perception, creating the awareness of being. This awareness exists in a dimensionless space. This perception is part of your being but you override it with thoughts and feelings. This is the deep inner quiet that allows you to feel connected to profound states of being. This energy creates space and light.

'The Unbroken Stone'
'Everlasting Flame'
'Lotus Light'
'The Buddha's Temple'

Electric Energy

The intensity of the atmosphere is so strong that currents of energy are formed, creating vitality and inspiration. These are electrical currents that follow the line of most intensity. The form is a subtle infusion of intensity and fluidity. This is the meeting point of the intangible with the physical. The intensity of the energy of the intangible brings life to the physical. It infuses every part of the physical body. This energy form is a fluid atmosphere, or positive radiation, that moves through and influences everything physical. It is a fluid conductor and support.

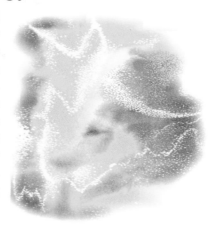

'Lion Heart'
'Light Forming'
'Pillar of Flame'
'Touching Earth'

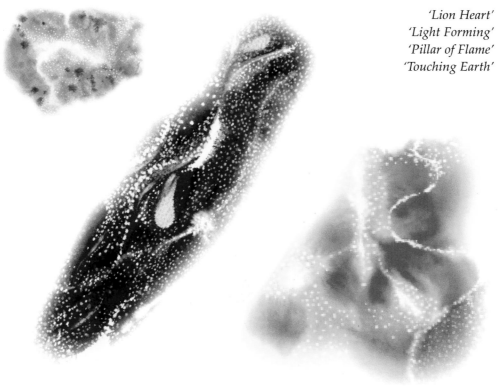

25

Unfolding Energy

Positive energy is generated and expanded producing visible effects, like flowers opening to the sun. There is a blossoming, fullness, and further growth. Enjoyment, happiness, and spiritual growth are the outcome.

'The Garden'
'Shining Out'

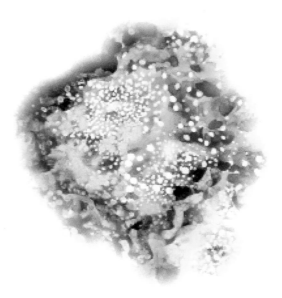

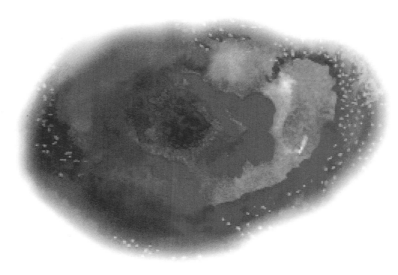

Expanding Energy

Light particles are created and formed from an intense energy, and released into their own space. This produces changes in the landscape and atmosphere, in a melting pot of creativity. This energy can be expansive or concentrated, and in each case fundamental changes will take place. This energy creates and releases particles of energy which form another type of energy. Much like ideas are formed, spoken-out as words, and then have their own effect.

'Creation'
'Constellations'

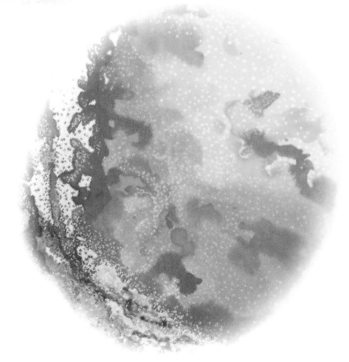

27

Dissolving Energy

This is a dynamic light energy breaking through a slower heavier energy. This energy dissolves an energy more solid than itself, like the heat of a volcano melting rocks, or the sea dissolving rock, or wind and rain eroding a mountain. Tiny particles of intense energy flow and blend, bringing light, movement, and change. The densest energy is dissolved and changed. The brightest areas are the most active, where explosive unpredictable energy is breaking through. This energy dissolves through constant activity.

'Incandescence'
'Light Energy'

Quiet Stable Energy

This energy is outside, and beyond, personal energy, as in an awareness of something that is beyond yourself. It exists in a spacious, uninterrupted, quiet. This quiet state can be imprinted with other energies, but they never upset the stable conditions. This may introduce a religious, spiritual, or historical perspective, into your life.

'Testament'
'Wonder'

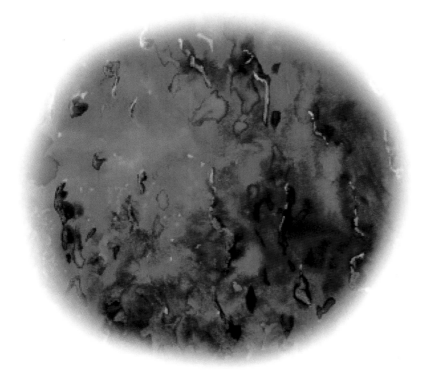

Keys Of Existence

Creation

The Tapestry Of Life

Pillar Of Flame

The Garden

Existence is formed, and made physical. You have a place in objective reality. This gives you your identity, perception, and awareness. Even though you are part of everything, it is also possible to see beyond into the void. You are guided by inspiration, and through awareness partake in everything. You have your place, or portion, on the Earth, which is full of possibilities.

Creation

Into Being

The spiritual is dropped into the ocean of the infinite, causing a chain reaction. An atom explodes or a new world is formed. Heat and light burst forth sending a wave of energy into the quiet, spacious, velvet night. There is plenty of room for all this to happen, and although the heat and light are powerful and dynamic, they have not in any way disturbed the peace and tranquillity of the night sky crescent. All of this activity is held in the crescent which gently flows around from indigo, into deep magenta, through soft pinks, into the heat and light. The centre radiates so much heat and light that it forms its' own atmosphere of tiny particles. Waves of energy gush out creating a new atmosphere of understanding. Dots of energy create a refraction of the light in rainbow waves. At the outer limits of this explosion of energy and awareness, yellow spiritual clouds tumble into the void. In that void other points of light can be seen going through the same process.

A new awareness of the ever-present creation is being formed. Creation is an endless awakening to the light. Things, animals, plants, and people, are coming into being all the time. The world is blossoming. Creation brings energy and awareness into form.

Awareness   Expansion   Peace

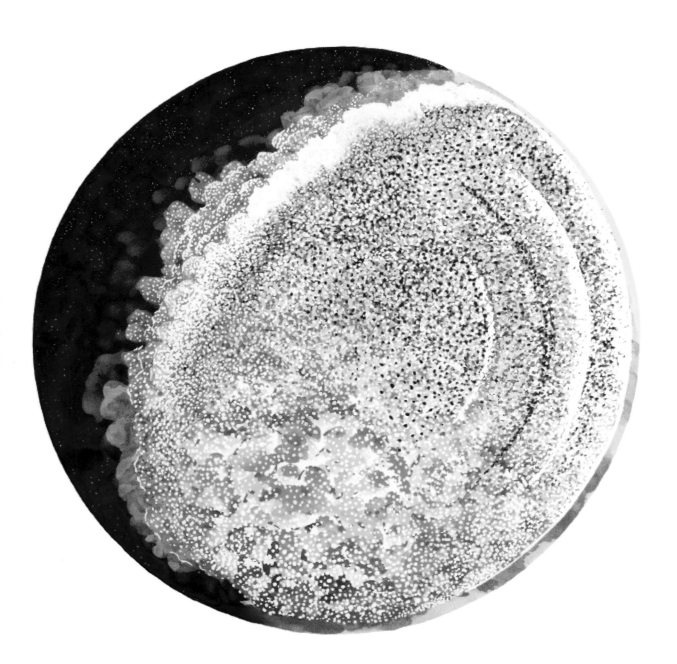

The Tapestry Of Life

'It's no accident that I'm here'

Strands are gently interwoven in the fabric of the universe, loosely like sacking, in a geometric pattern like a grid. The "grid" is like a city lit-up at night, teeming with life. The grid is everything.

There is a central diamond which appears darker. It is something other than the grid. There is a presence beyond your everyday preoccupations and involvements. You can see through gaps in the diamond, through pools of blue, into the starless void. The opposite of everything is nothing. This can appear terrifying at first, but it is only the opposite of everything. Everything is everything. Nothing is nothing. Do not confuse, or combine, the two. You look at nothing from everything. The known and the unknown.

Here is the interconnectedness of life that transcends time and space. "The fact that I am alive, I am connected". "My body, my life. This is me, I am here". The substance of your body is of the earth. Your identity is connected not only through time and place, but also other dimensions. This is the reassurance and connection of being part of a greater whole, having an identity and place in the world through the symbolic quality of tartan.

Connection   Identity   Assurance

Pillar Of Flame

Bringing thought to light

Ancient Knowing is revealed in a pillar of flame, bringing illumination that is timeless and impenetrable. Fire from Heaven brings inspiration down to Earth. The power of this downward energy reaching the Earth keeps your feet on the floor, whilst your head can reach up to the sky and see beyond.

Your thoughts follow a pattern unique to you. Your thoughts will reach conclusions according to these patterns of thought, experience, behaviour, and inheritance, and because they are restrained by this pattern of energy, they are closed to anything new. It is possible to leave these patterns once they have been recognised and acknowledged. There is then an openness to thoughts that are disconnected. They are created from spontaneous energy. They are new and light, and they bring in energy and vitality, insight and inspiration.

The downward movement of gold is a spiritual strength in the world. The stillness of magenta is power. The power of knowing ones' self. The purple is timeless and impenetrable. Its' depth is illuminated with gold and the feeling of silver, through the pinks, whites, and violets. The gold and silver add another kind of strength through movement and dynamic. A flow is created like a paisley pattern. The light of pinks, violets, blues and turquoise, electrify and change the energy of magenta. The magenta is given mobility by the electricity created from these colours. This is the illumination of being.

Illumination   Knowing   Revelation

The Garden

Allowing things to come to fruition

This is just one portion of a landscape of trees and rivers, or a view through an orchard in full bloom. This is a primordial Garden of Eden. Even though apparently deserted, here is richness and depth. The spiritual glow of yellow is subdued and diverted by the downward triangle to form a relaxed identity in the world. To this is added magenta rose creating a different energy to move things along. The downward triangle gives direction and allows things to come to fruition without effort. The two downward edges form a boundary, but the top of the triangle is open and continuous. In the deeper blues and greens stability is introduced, and we can now see movement and activity, and light, like seeing the stars by daylight. This scene is teeming with life.

As well as your generosity and helpful input there is growth and change, but these come about in their own time. As soon as something comes into being, the timing of events happen according to the intangible world, and you can allow things to come to fruition naturally. This is the "Garden of the Heart." "Summer and her fullness."

Happiness   Abundance   Stability

40

Keys Of Generating Energy

Shining Out

Incandescence

Touching Earth

Lion Heart

You occupy this physical world as a dynamic presence, but beyond the physical appearance of things, and all thought, is an energy. This is the flow of energy as a movement or dynamic that gives you life, and which you can access. You are connected to this energy through your heart. The heart is a container of energy, which overflows to give life. It inspires, and powers-up your physical body, moves thoughts and feelings, and lets you glimpse the profound. You are inspired into life by energy. From a physical energy and presence, awareness is born into the world.

Shining Out

'Man cannot live by Red alone'

You are here and occupy this space through colour, and energy. Red is at the root of this spectrum of colour, and it is needed to express yourself here in the world. Red is the physical manifestation of being here. Red drives the world through expression. This is your physical presence.

Red is actually the physical space, which you occupy. Red brings things about. However, red must dominate, and each person, and each thing on Earth, will exercise this power. Creation and destruction go on through red alone, and you live in a physical world of red. The creative aspects are tremendous, but the misunderstanding is that you could live by red alone. There is a strong need by red to dominate. Red is red. This is its' power and its' purpose.

Enjoy your red. Red is powerful. Exercise the power. Celebrate the red. Put another way, celebrate your life. Red is at the root of this physical life, alive and dynamic. Red is the celebration of being physically alive. Uplifting golden dots of movement keep the red clouds active and alive. When red becomes static it looses its vitality, its' brightness fades, and it slips into brown. When something happens to take your vitality away, such as a deliberate action, or criticism, by someone else, your brightness can fade and move into the brown of resentment, like dead blood. For some, the absence of bright red, mostly through fear, or apology, will lead to feelings of inadequacy or resentment. This is a fear of your own physical dominance, which may appear cruel, insensitive, or entirely physical and material. These are the words of the apology. You cannot be fulfilled or live comfortably without red. Red is the statement "I will do what I will do". This inevitably causes a reaction in the red of every other person, and is just another reason for withdrawal or nonaction.

Physical life is a manifestation of spirit. This is the heart of the matter. You cannot live by red alone, because there is more to life than ego, status, and power. You cannot live by the physical alone. Red is a statement of your movement and vitality. This is the joy of being yourself, and a celebration of being alive. Your physical presence here gives you the right to be as you are.

Nourishing   Expression   Uplifting

Incandescence

Glad to find your fears groundless

The present and persistent energies of thoughts and concerns, of disappointments and beliefs, can be changed. Through a change of view, understanding comes when you realise that your insights and intuitions can guide you away from heavier thoughts and emotions. Becoming aware of the intangible energies gives you a new perspective on life. It is a relief to not have to take everything so seriously. Not having to be assertive or right creates openness to change. Change and letting-go are welcomed.

There is the presence of too much red, but this is moved and changed by yellow and white energy breaking through as heat. The red being heavier than yellow, is melted by the dissolving power of yellow. Focus is brought back into the red as the molten yellow breaks-through lower down. The yellow flows down, dissolving the red. A dynamic balance is achieved between the red physical and material power, and the introduction of yellow non-material or spiritual energy. Light awareness brings an end to heavy disappointment.

Focus   Change   Transformation

44

Touching Earth

This heart, this life

This is the energy of the heart and its connection with the organs of the physical body bringing life and nourishment. The hearts' energy connects through the physical heart to your life experiences here. The heart rests in an energy of reflective liquid golden yellow. It has a metallic quality that adds power to the reflecting light, creating an electrical fluidity. It is very sensitive to all energies. The yellow is life-giving and reflectively protecting. Electromagnetic white strikes of energy bring everything to life. This is good health.

The heart itself is a vessel that is full and overflowing with energy. This overflow infuses the physical body with life and everything is expressed through the heart. It is for this reason that the heart is vulnerable. Your heart is the centre of your life. You begin with your heart, and things affect your heart first. Your heart is a receptor and regulator. It is a driving force of direction. The heart rests within a thin white line that forms a diamond. This line is so thin and light it allows flexibility, strength and protection. Everything can flow, nothing is fixed. The top and bottom of the diamond connect to your life line, which anchors you in place in this heart, in this life, now.

Reflective   Sensitivity   Fluidity

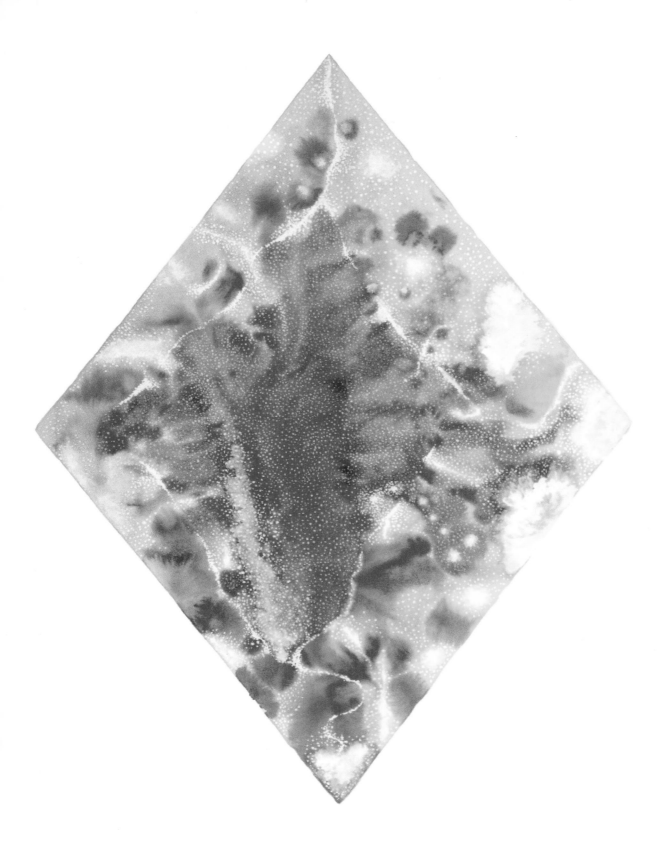

Lion Heart

"I am alive"

The softness and receptivity of the heart is inspired by yellow. The yellow is so intense, that it has become electrified. Currents of white electricity are formed within the magnetic energy of the yellow atmosphere. They draw upon, and make contact with, the stronger earth energy of orange, electrifying the heart, bringing it to life. The heart generates warmth and light and an explosion of creativity, optimism, and potential. The electric white is breaking through the orange boundary into new fields of activity.

From a physical presence something else has happened. From the hearts' centre spiritual awareness and insight bursts forth and enters the world. "Yes! I am alive". "Realising it, I act on it. I am aware, and I am open to endless possibilities. I am free to choose, and to look and listen. My life is the source of awareness and wonder. I have arrived !"

Inspiration   Receptivity   Vitality

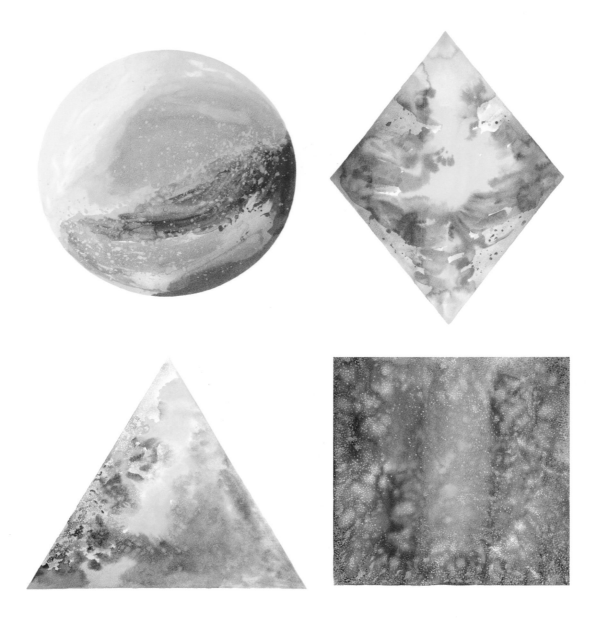

Keys Of Perception

Beautiful World

Angel

Light Energy

Expansion

There are lots of subtle steps in your perception, from inner and outer activity which brings satisfaction and involvement, to expanding your awareness out to where everything appears still and motionless. Awareness goes beyond perception, in a process that continues endlessly between states of awake and dream life. Behind everything is an intangible energy, and it influences everything. This energy is your connection to earth, and an awareness of different dimensions.

Beautiful World

Revealing Wonder

Here is a view of a planet from space that looks still and motionless. Like the Earth turning, things are in fact moving and changing. High above the clouds, the white energy of the universe is waiting to be absorbed into the atmosphere. You can look through and move closer to the surface. Under the blanket of soft yellow clouds there is a world to discover. As you move through this world you can hear things and feel its' activity and involvement. You could become part of it.

There is a satisfaction to be found in the everyday world around you, by being open to what is on offer. Everything is provided and you can enjoy it on your own level. There is satisfaction in yellow, and a sweetness in pink. Combined they produce enjoyment. Pink is vitality, variety, diversity, and wonder. This is the freshness of the morning, the colour, light, and vibrancy of the world, which you can only see if you look straight through, or beyond, your own attitude. You use your attitude to filter everything. An attitude isn't necessary. When it's left behind, satisfaction and wonder are revealed.

Revealed through yellow is pink, opaque and translucent, open to the music of the universe. The yellow dissolves to reveal a new wonder beneath. It is as though beautiful yellow wasn't enough, and that there is an even greater wonder behind it, powering it up. Beyond your busy involvement in the world, is another dimension and experience. Waking afresh everyday to the wonder.

Satisfaction   Enjoyment   New

Angel

Dream takes form

You dream yourself alive, and that dreaming doesn't stop when you are born. It continues. Your whole existence is a continuance of dreaming. You create the person that you are, and as your understanding changes, you change. What you know takes form, and you are the form of your own awareness.

Yellow dreams itself alive and comes into being. Pink is the energy of the dream, and the yellow is absorbed into it. The clear space of the translucent pink gives it plenty of room to do this, in its' own time, and in its' own special way. Where these two energies, of awareness and being, meet, vitality is formed as orange. This vitality is pure untarnished energy.

Yellow infuses the physical on the deepest levels, like a baby forming in the womb. You can see the main fabric of the body, the skull and spine, and the muscles, formed before emergence. At one stage this is an angel in the intangible realms of pure energy and colour. Later, the physical will dominate, and colour and energy will seem to loose their connection. Ribs, like wings, are connected to a flow and movement that will later be confirmed by the breath. In this flow of the breath is your connection to the spiritual. There is a wondrous connection between your awareness and this flow. This goes on without thought. It happens on its own.

All of this rests in a dreamtime of far greater awareness than the physical body itself. You have never moved out of the dreamtime. You rest in the physical, while not being part of it. The dream is eternal. You are continually, now, all the time, coming into being.

Dreaming   Openness   Peacefulness

54

Light Energy

Bringing your light into the world

Through acceptance (without thoughts or opinions) and letting-go you can find stability and comfort in even the most active and involved circumstances. 'The Softening Process' is free of ego, and continues without thought. Naturally and effortlessly it dissolves, expanding out into the universe. Yellow melts and dissolves into two different elements. The pink of being and knowing expands out into the uncharted blues and turquoise, while the reds, greens, and purples create light and energy, enthusiasm, and happiness, as though through thousands of points of light.

The opposite elements of quiet awareness and discovery, and the energetic power of action and expression, both exist side by side. In a world of opposites you don't need to promote one or the other, to prove or disprove, to explain or justify. You can live in a world of opposites without prejudice, knowing the world is full of opposites and opportunities. You are free to live and breathe, and at the same time relaxing in the world, you become energised, blending with the universe.

Dissolving   Effortless   Accepting

Expansion

Seeing what is

Clouds of yellow move outward, expanding and dissolving. The clouds seem to rest in a space above the reflective violet. The violet does not attract, but provides a still space on which things can glide. The violet energy is so reflective it influences the energies around it, causing them to slip and melt, dissolve and move freely, creating relaxation. This is the inner space in which there is no surface on which thought can get a purchase. Although it is deep and fathomless, it provides assurance. It's like being able to see clearly when everything is relaxed.

Everything is as it is, but it is difficult to see it without associations, opinions, and preferences, getting in the way. When you look you push-out your view onto the world, agreeing or disagreeing. 'Seeing what is' is just observing. Your awareness is not confined by physical or mental parameters. It is free to move and expand in a space that is physical and intangible. Your awareness can blend and become part of anything. Just look and listen to what is presented, for the world is surprising, and enlightening.

Clarity   Space   Occupy

Keys Of Purity

Wonder

Soundless Space

Testament

The Prayer Wheel

The world is alive with wonder, full of profound and mysterious things, and it is easy to become lost in the wonder. Everything is pure in itself, and by seeing the wonder you become part of it. If you leave your thoughts and concepts behind, you can see and find the wonder and purity in each thing, and marvel at it. You are here in this world, but it has other dimensions. The two states, of the ordinary world and the profound wonder, co-exist at the same time. It is for you to see the wonder. Your own presence here is a wonder, and you remain open to wonder. Wonder is without thought. It creates a space or a place in itself. A spiritual and physical relationship is formed between you and this world, and this life.

You can enter into the wonder through the natural world, weather and light, or through prayer. Prayer is a living state that you enter into. Prayer is an access into wonder. Purity is the expression and appreciation of wonder.

Wonder

The Great Mystery

Within the greens of nature, from the dark blue greens to light yellow greens, are all the living energies. As the greens move into olive green a link to gold is created. It is as though deep in the Earth seams of gold are to be found in the most earthy of greens. This is the purity of Earth. Within olive green is peace on Earth. This is our connection with Earth.

This is an upward triangle but the flow of energy is slow and measured like a solution dissolving in water. It flows downward, creating a solid stable foundation. The apple green border lets in the right amount of light and influence. The green itself says what light can enter. Here the energy is like a wood. When you step into the wood, you enter the world of green. Everything around you is alive, and the further in you go, the deeper the mystery. "Being alive in a place that is itself alive, moving through in three dimensions. Alive but not alone. Alive Here, in a great mystery."

Even though we aspire to ascend, the spiritual can be found in the Earth itself. The spiritual infuses everything. There is a 'wonder' to everything here and we can feel the effect. We have feeling and intuition which can move us deeper. This profound feeling stirs the emotions, and disrupts thoughts, as we perceive The Great Mystery.

Physical   Autonomy   Vigour

Soundless Space

Enough room for you

Cream dots of energy fall like snow in the quiet of a pine forest. Nothing stirs. In this deep pine forest you could 'loose yourself' to the wonder, and forget everything else. The falling snow and the softness and quiet depth of the forest form a marriage of two different types of quiet. There is the energy of falling snow in lightness and movement, without sound, and the branches of the trees as a presence, colour and softness, without movement. Sound isn't necessary for things to happen. This absence of sound creates immense space and scale. Here is softness and depth, movement and space.

Listening and receiving without sound allows you to go within to that place where you just are. It is like allowing yourself to sink into yourself without having to keep up appearances. This soundless energy allows you to let go of behaving in a way that only pleases others, or doing what others expect. It allows you to softly let go of tensions and worldly responsibilities and restrictions. There is enough room for you to look around, go at your own pace, and do things in your own way. You can be here, just as you are. You are here in the world, in the body you are in, but this location has other dimensions.

Release   Stillness   Place

Testament

The story of your life

The tablet contains the writing of your life. A writing of the history of individual existence. Each person has one of these tablets, completed in their lifetime. There is a spiritual dimension to everyday life and your relationship with everyone and everything else. While you are here, you have been given this body and all of these earthly connections. You live them out through time, building on them, and refining them. Through purpose and connection, intention and significance, you live and share the story of your life.

Within the rich browns and dark greens of Earth gold is forming. The pure gold is strong and untarnished. This is the purity of Earth. Here, gold is part of the greens as a witness of life. The darks are timeless and bring calm stability. The emotions are settled, gaining a sense of place, and a level of comfort and peace. There is light here, bursting softly through the still pale yellow and apple greens. "You have a life here".

Witness   Acknowledgement   Virtue

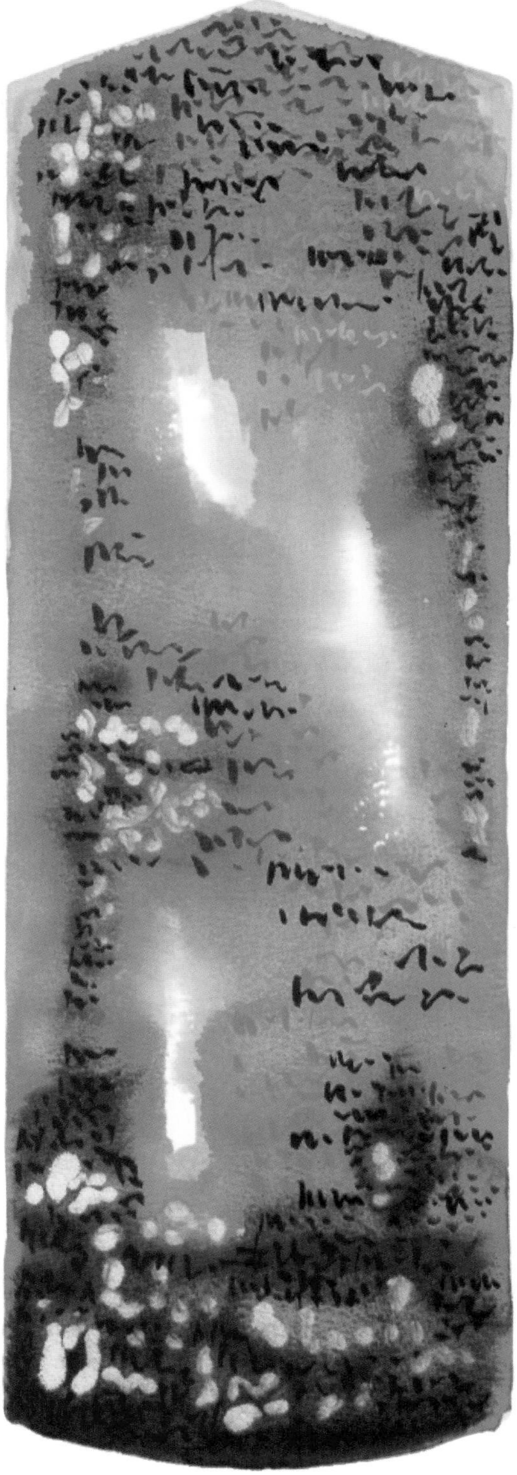

The Prayer Wheel

Stepping into

Light reflected from the gold gives a three-dimensional feeling. There is also a soft translucent quality, as though you could move through into another world inside the sphere. The surface is covered with ancient writing of every prayer that has ever been said, is being said, and will ever be said. The same questions and the same prayers are asked over time. It is in the asking of these prayers that the sharing of the spiritual takes place. Human awareness goes through the same unfolding whatever time a person lives in, past, present, or future. Prayer is a state that you enter into.

We are always stepping into different states, different light, different weather, different atmospheres, and different places. When you are aware of, and accept, stepping into changing conditions, it enhances your awareness.

Profound   Knowing   Enter

70

Keys Of Acceptance

Living In The Clouds

Forgiveness

Pearl

Lotus Light

By simply accepting yourself and your own way of life, you can appreciate your place in the world. There is no right or wrong way, and there is no need to suffer other peoples' opinion or blame. However, your attention may be caught by the ordinary world, and there could be disappointment. When you recognise and accept the state of the world as it is, you can let go of it. There is no need to resort to experience, explanation, dissatisfaction, or disappointment. This is an acceptance of the fact that you have a right to your own freedom. By being open, without having to impress, or apologise to, others, you can accept your own place and potential in the world. The world does not need your attention all the time. You are allowed to imagine, to daydream, and to relax. From being quiet, a natural state of stillness, clarity, and creativity, emerges. This quiet state is close to the source of your spiritual being.

Living In The Clouds

Softening

This is a strange view, high up in the clouds, unconnected to reality. Clouds shift, move, and roll, over a mirrored green background. This ground underneath is intense, reflective and slippery, like electrical energy. It is a shiny surface with no dimensions.

The clouds contain turquoise, pink, and yellow, which reveal other qualities reflected from the heavens. The cloud forms are expansive and are the opposite of reason, seriousness, coercion and control. These are the comforting clouds of acceptance. They reflect the light and bring in movement and transformation in a subtle, soft, acceptable way. These clouds allow transformation from a negative, holding, or stressful, state, to being open, and accepting change. This is the answer to the pull of conformity or convention and the need to hold on, prove, or demonstrate. The clouds relax emotional tension and bring in space, light, and relaxation. The orange corners define or make us aware of an overview, to bring focus and adjustment, and put things into perspective.

Any stressful situation demands more attention, and your thoughts are unable to escape this cycle. By moving your attention to the ever-present clouds you are immediately removed from the cycle into a comfortable, comforting place. Relax into soft clouds while the world turns by itself. Once you understand this principle you can go to the clouds at any time, and for no reason. Your worldly thoughts can dominate your life, but they are only a small part of you. Beyond or above these thoughts you have your own sensitivity, your own awareness, and your own peaceful state that is open to the world. This is 'The Softening Process', and it goes much further.

Relaxation   Comfort   Openness

Forgiveness

Radiance not obedience

A spiritual light infuses the clouds as though a whole world is created above the Earth. This is not the habitat of angels or heavenly hosts, but an aware state of freedom and acceptance available to all. At the highest point is peace and clarity. Pinks and yellows deepen to provide cover, comfort, and protection. A celestial authority seems to come from above, or be directed downward, but as the clouds gather in volume they reflect back the light and there is a radiance everywhere. The energy is spread, shared, increased and deepened. This brings-in balance and harmony, and gentle change.

This is the resolution of overpowering authority. Freedom from oppression cannot be found in conflict or compromise. The clouds are the opposite energy to the line of no compromise which seeks to overpower anything in its' way. Forgiveness is not a grand statement, an apology, or re-consideration of memory, but an act of pure light and softening. The softening process has the power to move and change all things. It is the changing of your own view, through a forgiveness, that creates freedom from oppression. It is the light itself that gives strength, rather than obedience to it.

Accumulation   Softening   Freedom

Pearl

Deeper peace

This celestial scene lifts you into another dimension. A luminous light draws you in. There is a calmness, dreaminess, and clarity, that creates an overall effect of tranquillity, and the feeling of moving through deeper peaceful states.

Harmony is achieved through the strength of orange which emanates from the golden yellow as softness and acceptance, and the quietness of the soft blues and violets which allow reflection and contemplation. Orange is the joy of being, in a sea of blue contentment. The violet rim of the circle is clarity. The pinks and violets are restful, imaginative, and otherworldly. The golden light of the yellow blends with the blue, turning it to the gentle green of stillness. The clouds link with these colours reflecting the light. This creates a rainbow effect.

The appearance is of tranquillity, but within this is a powerful spiritual awareness. Optimism has an expanding influence. This is the balance of softness and strength, brightness and subtlety, movement and stillness, that is revitalising and energising.

Balance   Calming   Creative

Lotus Light

The Source

Soft golden petals emanate from a white core, and dream longer petals of white breezes. Some flow upward, like flames, others flow downward, folding and forming a cushion with the turquoise on which the golden flower rests. There is limitless space here, and deeper still, behind the drifting clouds, there are white stars, still and bright. Each of these stars is a 'Lotus Light', and you are looking closely at one of them.

This is the state of pure awareness, in which there is nothing else to do, or to correct. In the material world anything may look unfinished, or there may be the idea that something more could be done, or that something is missing. There will always be something to do, but things are always as they are.

Here is balance and harmony. Through your sensitivity there is an acceptance, and a softening of your involved control, which allows you to occupy your own space. Acceptance is a state of openness, even though your thoughts continue and there is always something else. By realising that your thoughts are 'the something else', you begin to be open. This sensitivity is the source of your being. It gives light, fullness, and awareness. This is a spiritual state that unfolds here.

Emanation   Subtlety   Sensitivity

Keys Of Being Here

The Buddha's Temple

The Winged Dragon

The Untarnished Shield

The Theatre Of Life

At this moment, being here now is all there is. This here, now, is the meeting place of the tangible and the intangible. Energy is movement and change, and the motive force behind all things. Chance, change, and new possibilities, are introduced all the time. You are at the centre of all this movement and change. There is a stability from being constant in the perpetual movement of the world. By remaining on the surface of things, without pressure or over-involvement, you can see your way clearly and express yourself. While you are here you have been given this body and situation. It is your life for you. Your sensitivity and imagination are gifts to be used. While you are here, express yourself. Everyday that you are here is a celebration of life.

The Buddha's Temple

Residing in the physical

There is a close connection between the substance of the Earth and your physical body. The Earth is impermanent, but always present, as you are.

From the deep red and crimson, yellow bursts through like natural springs flowing from the Earth. Two pillars bring balance and strength into the movement and heat of orange. Place and time act as the solid foundation and stability of the Earth. These two pillars bring energy from deep within the Earth and make a connection with your heart. The heart is fuelled by understanding and expressed here on Earth.

White lightening energy is sent downward from the heavens to give inspiration, insight and wisdom. The Buddha's Temple on Earth connects you with intangible spiritual forces. What you make on Earth is from the earth, and what you aspire to is from heaven. The meeting of two different energy flows within you produces a dynamic energy or the spirit incarnated, like an Indian deity carved in stone. You are here now. This is the acceptance of physical earthly life here, without fear, and a celebration of spirit.

Substance   Stability   Affinity

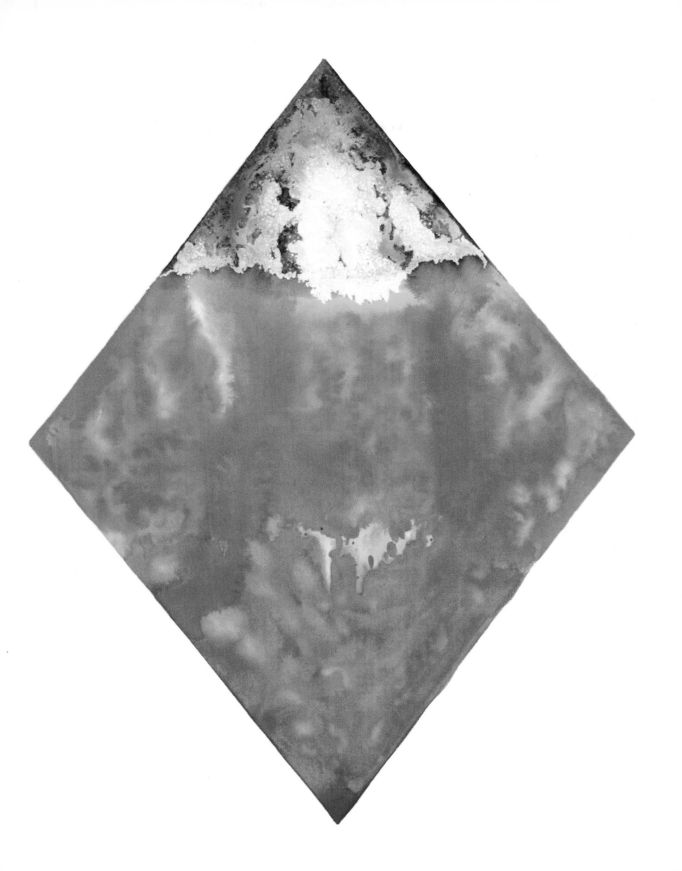

The Winged Dragon

New possibilities

Two powerful assertive colours, of blue and orange, compete, or, through understanding, combine. The blue dragon is uncompromising, single minded, and intentional. The luminescence of the orange creates a warm confidence. The blue pushes through the expansive orange, but cannot overpower it. As the blue lets go of its' reaction, clouds begin to form, cushioning the intensity of each colour, allowing the blue energy to flow up and outward. This is the freeing of energy through a combination of understanding, confidence, and intention.

Originally the dragon had form, and bright feathers that reacted with the orange, forming stressful tangled connections and an unnecessary flamboyance in a competitive atmosphere. As the feathers disappeared the clouds formed, releasing the dragon, allowing it to become lighter, to fly, and blend with the universe. It is possible to achieve your aims in a quiet confidence without the need to push or over-assert yourself. The dragons' path is directed by the cushioning clouds as it flows through the orange, creating a new universe.

The universe expands to incorporate new stars and galaxies. The deeper colours indicate physical states in a process of change over aeons of time, and the reds, greens, and turquoise, introduce variety, evolution, and change. Change brings new possibilities. Every day something new is created, thought, discovered, and experienced. In this vast scheme of things you get another go, endlessly.

Confidence   Intention   Potential

The Untarnished Shield

The strength of seeing

Sometimes the surface reality of our lives is so reflective that it feels like thick glass. You could look through the glass, like the refracting surfaces of the lens of a lighthouse. The inner light of the lighthouse is reflected outwards through the prismatic effect onto the world, and remains untarnished as it is constantly renewed by movement.

The speed is like a spinning top which keeps its' balance and place, not as a vortex, but as a series of concentric circles, which allows energy to spin always in the present. This is expressing yourself now in the present moment. Underneath the surface there are different depths and temperatures, like moods, but the fast speed keeps you on the surface. The surface reflects, and shines, your identity and individuality, and its' speed and strength feels refreshing and energising.

You can look down through the centre, like a well, where it is calm and still. The centre is enlivening.

Constancy   Lucid   Centred

The Theatre Of Life

Your world

A magical flourish of colour like a children's cardboard theatre. This is the joy of expression and imagination. At the yellow centre there is room to expand, and change the scene, in an atmosphere of fun and happiness. It's all 'child's play'.

But this 'child's play' is about positive expanding energy, that gives you more vitality, interest, and enjoyment. There may well be a serious, even negative, view in the world, but there is more to life, and yourself. This is not about your own personal viewpoint, since that viewpoint is merely a reflection of tired, but tried and tested, old holding energy. There are millions and millions of viewpoints in the world, each one to do with a person's own inner world and experience. You have been brought-up, educated, and instinctively know, that this viewpoint is not only necessary to get through life, but essential. Without it, you are told that you would be lost. Everything you come into contact with is seen, filtered, and judged, through your viewpoint. It is your viewpoint that causes all the problems, not the world with its' endless challenges and opportunities. No one (viewpoint) can ever have the correct view since the world is open to everything. Everything is going on.

When you play you can live without the intrusion of feelings of insecurity, fitting-in, or responsibility, and expand out into the world, without fear, compromise, or worrying about the reaction. Life is a big presentation, and you step out onto the stage. Things do happen between the stage and the audience, but all the action takes place on the stage, with you. At some point you created an attitude, reacted, took on a role, or took it seriously, and forgot about the play and the childrens' theatre, even though the sun comes out every morning and lights everything up.

Yellow and orange have burst forth from the centre, over the pink edges of the stage. They cannot be contained and the colours pour out, like the petals of a flower, gaining strength and momentum. Green appears as choice, bringing more strength and definition, and white energy brings, speed, activity, and expression. You have control, and an overview and perspective, of the story of your life. You move things around, and you determine the story.

In all your life, make it interesting, colourful, and imaginative. The world is here for you. You have been born into it, and are here to play, and adventure in it. You are here, and you are cast in the play.

Play   Choice   Zest

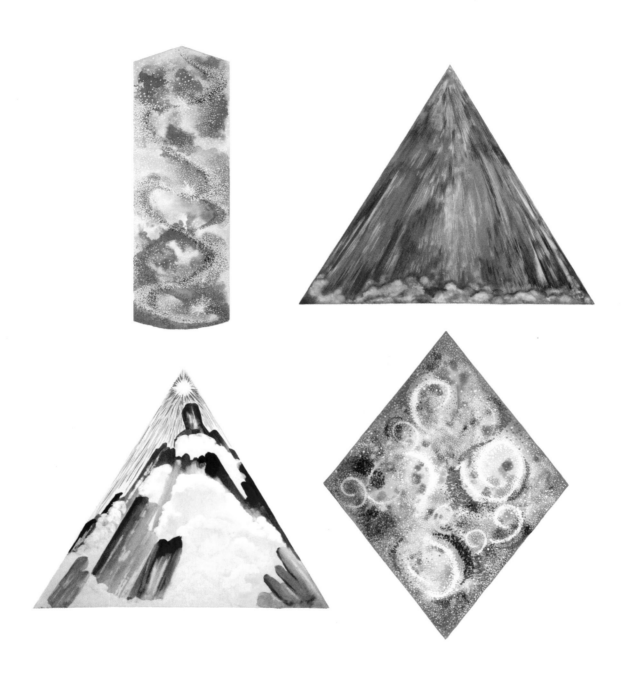

Keys Of Self

Contact

Behind The Veil

The Guiding Star

Cornucopia

There is a natural spring of energy that rises from the Earth. It is a fountain of expression and awareness. You move upward through intuition and inspiration to an awareness of your own inner guidance. At the highest point is your guiding star, which leads to the realisation that you are blessed. Your energy and inner strength guides you, and can be expressed fully in the world.

Contact

The Natural Spring

There are three stars in human evolution. The first star, in a field of red, is conception. This is the star of 'Recognition' and action. It states "I am here". It is an affirmation made by everyone, in response to their nature, and place, in the world.

There are two spirals of energy that climb upward. One is orange-red and the other is blue-green. The physical orange-red is heavy Earth energy and has a limit to how high it can rise. As you walk there is an energizing contact, through your feet, with the Earth. This energy travels upward bringing-in vitality and good health. This is the natural spring. It reaches the second star of 'Action', but after that its' form and direction dissolves if it cannot change colour. The blue-green spiral is self-awareness and knowing, and it continues upward into unknown regions. This life-line continues beyond the physical, as far as you can imagine, and further. Beyond that, and further still, the natural spring of life continues.

The second star is potential and intention, where the physical and material are combined and empowered. This makes the statement "I can". The vital source of energy continues to rise up through, and out of, the physical, moving free, vibrant and unrestrained.

The third star of 'Realisation' shines brightly, lighting-up the orange-red. This star makes the statement "I am". This is the introduction of spiritual energy, through insight, inspiration, and imagination, which continues rising out of the physical shell.

Celebration   Continuity   Breakthrough

Behind The Veil

Your own authority

The flow of energy is like a waterfall. The water is clean and clear. The softest energy is at the centre, as though falling in slow motion. The outer edges are very fast, creating the illusion of glass or a veil. It is like looking through a waterfall. The fall of the water is very powerful and it's difficult to see anything except the speed and power of the water.

It is as if the falling water forms the garments of a figure, his face obscured from view. It is the figure of authority, which each person must recognise for themselves. This is in fact your own authority, obscured from view. Can you stand-up to this figure ? A hand can be seen at the top left. Does the hand beckon you to move forward through the waterfall ? Does it give you the 'thumbs up', or does it say "go no further", or "go away"? The lines of energy flow downward, but the energy of the figure behind beckons you upward. At the apex, in deep turquoise, it is still and centred. This is where the power is, and everything else is a show or demonstration. This is the inner quiet ability to excerpt your own influence and authority.

Decision   Voice   Recognition

The Guiding Star

Inner strength

Earth energy is raising itself up to the highest point. Crystal forms push their way upwards, from deep in the earth, up through the clouds. You can see light through the purity of the crystals. Sensitivity is crystallised as intuition, and cushioned by the clouds. As you move into this sensitivity there is a clarity like being in the clear air of the Himalayas. Through the clarity and spaciousness you are inspired. You reach up with your mind, through intention and a conscious opening of awareness, to translate sensitivity into information.

At the highest point is the clearest air. This is the highest point on Earth, and is a place of peace and clarity, where the influence of Heaven is felt most clearly. The light is different, and the air is different. Here is a balance of physical movement and strength with softness and intuition.

The bright star of white light at the apex is your guiding star. This is the presence of something else, beyond your material and mental life, like the sun which aids your willing progress. You need to be open to the presence and intangible support this offers, through intuition, the realisation of greater possibilities, and spiritual insight. Above the Earth and beyond the clouds there is the warm glow of silence and radiating energy which leads to the realisation that you are blessed.

Blessings   Independence   Certainty

Cornucopia

Greater depth

You have the strength of a diamond, bounded by the orange of being here, alive. Inside you, your energy or intention fizzles like fireworks, or unfolds like the opening of a fern leaf. A paisley pattern of white energies are unfolding, letting go, and dissolving. Thoughts are dissolving, making light energy. The white energy stirs-up everything, creating diversity, variety, and excitement. The orange diamond contains all of these dimensions and movements of energy. This inner life is expressed in the world. This confidence of living, and dissolving thoughts, creates abundance. Living life to the full.

Productive   Exuberance   Inventive

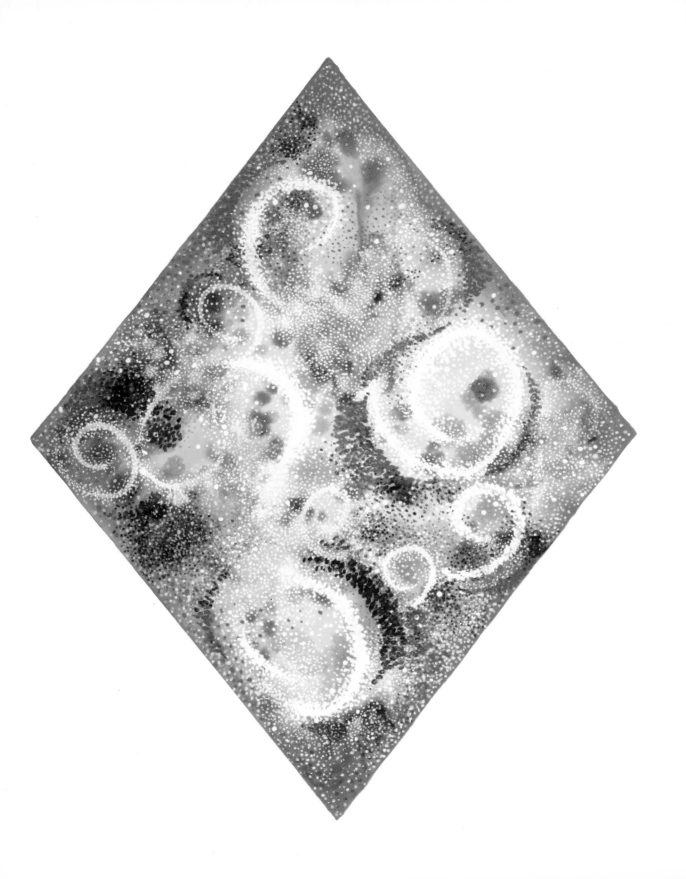

Keys Of Continuity

Constellations

The Seasons

Everlasting Flame

The Unbroken Stone

Appearances and action are formed out of the intangible. By being open and receptive to ideas they can become real in the world. You are at the centre, and everything revolves around you. Being at the centre of it all, your perception rests in this everlasting state, which has a timeless quality. It is a part of you, and also a place where your essential being resides. Continuity is an everlasting state that you can become aware of. Open to what else might come along, you are alive to something else, and a more subtle dimension or awareness.

Constellations

Ideas forming

The balance of fire and water, formless and full of energy. Movement and change move through the formless. Ideas and action appear, or are brought about by each other. In the world, it seems as if ideas are "heated up", when they are brought into the physical, used, and made real, or spoken-out as words. If you look again you can see the clockwise direction from an active state (the warm yellows, orange, and red) to another cooler, quieter, state (blues and magentas), which is more open. This open, intuitive, state is with us all the time, but the eruption of activity, from within, brings about movement and change.

Yellow is the hottest colour, which cools into orange and red. In this process it expands out into the blue, where it cools further, moving from orange to deep red, and then into soft pinks and violet, and turquoise comes into being. The yellows (intellect), orange (social and emotional), and reds (passion and commitment), create the energy for involvement and physical action. When this energy is sufficiently cooled or slowed-down, it is transformed into the higher frequencies of the pinks, turquoise, and violets, linking it to the creativity of the imagination. This quiet state provides intuition, insights, and guidance.

Ancients looked up to the heavens and drew imaginary outlines, connecting fixed stars to show the influence of the heavens on earth. This was the influence of ideas, of seeing signs and interpreting them, and out of this, belief systems were formed. Thoughts are formed all the time. They come into being, and you follow their pattern and express them in the world. They come out of the intangible, and are expressed, or dissolve back into the intangible.

Intuition   Insights   Guidance

The Seasons

Being present

Looking up into the canopy of tall trees, seeing the light filtering through the leaves coming down to Earth. The Earth moves on its axis creating the seasons. Great calendars were formed to connect you to this place and its' changing seasons. Looking upward at the night sky through a telescope you can observe the vastness of the heavens, beyond your earthly life. This is about seeing the wonder of your place in the scheme of things, and being at its' centre.

There is a stabilizing quality like a gyroscope spinning on its' axis, free to turn, and yet maintaining a fixed direction in any situation. Whatever change happens, you can observe on all levels, spiritually, mentally, emotionally, and physically. This way of seeing the world, its' changing seasons, day and night, different weathers, changing light, is 'the wonder'. This has a timeless quality, beyond history or place. This is perception without thought, which is boundless, and yet part of everything. Everything revolves around you. The wonder is found in change and stillness, and through these you expand your awareness.

Experience   Presence   Observation

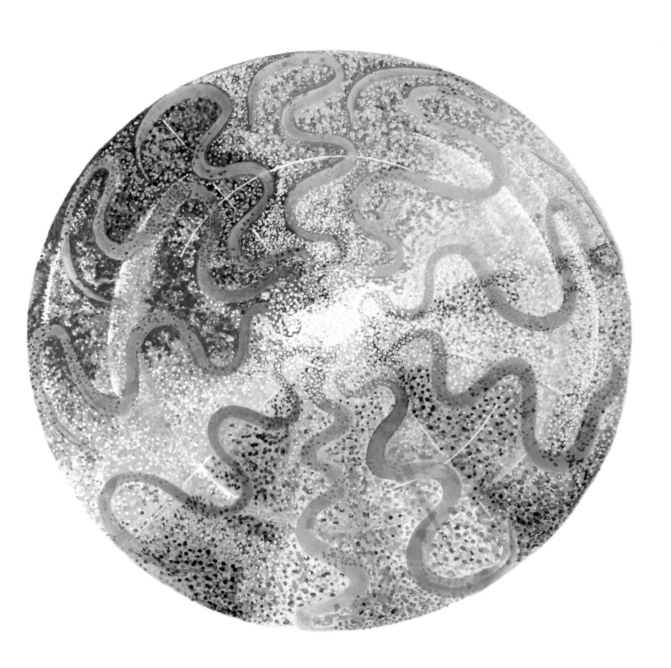

Everlasting Flame

Interwoven through time

The brightness and warmth of orange and gold. Fireside stories, warmth and company, in the protection of the earth. Sharing stories, anyone can identify with heroes and adventures. Shadow play of flames on lit walls. Flames leap up for a moment and disappear. If you listen closely you can hear the crackling of the fire. Sparks fly out and mark time in the ethereal gold and yellow.

Here the flame is white and the space, room, or ambience, is orange. The space has taken on the warmth and qualities of fire, and the fire is pure untarnished everlasting white. This is the everlasting flame. All things emanate from the flame. It tells the story and we observe age-old patterns, that are the same now as they were at the beginning of time. Each thing has its' presence now. The fire consumes everything, and yet we want to record the fleeting thing, event, or experience. All things are connected through time, and you too have your place in time.

Safety   Belonging   Sharing

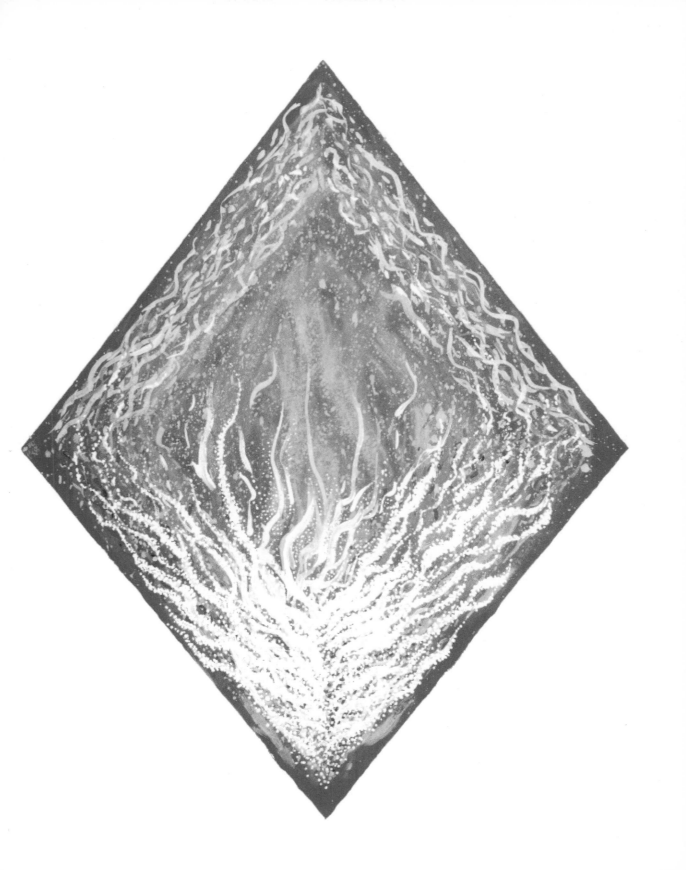

The Unbroken Stone

The Living Fire

The unbroken stone is a seam that runs uninterrupted through the Earth. The physical body is a theme that runs through time, like the history of a people painted on rock, or printed on fabric, like batik.

A wave of energy fans-out like peacock feathers, giving the feeling of a breeze, to tell the story of perception through the same individual through time. The breeze becomes a strong wind and its' colour changes from soft pink to strong blue. In this blue energy, the golden eyes in the peacock feathers are like galaxies or looking through into different worlds. In this shimmering golden atmosphere the white flames of perception are a focus of listening, seeing, and stillness. This is carried on the energy of the wind like a living fire.

Listening   Stillness   Focus

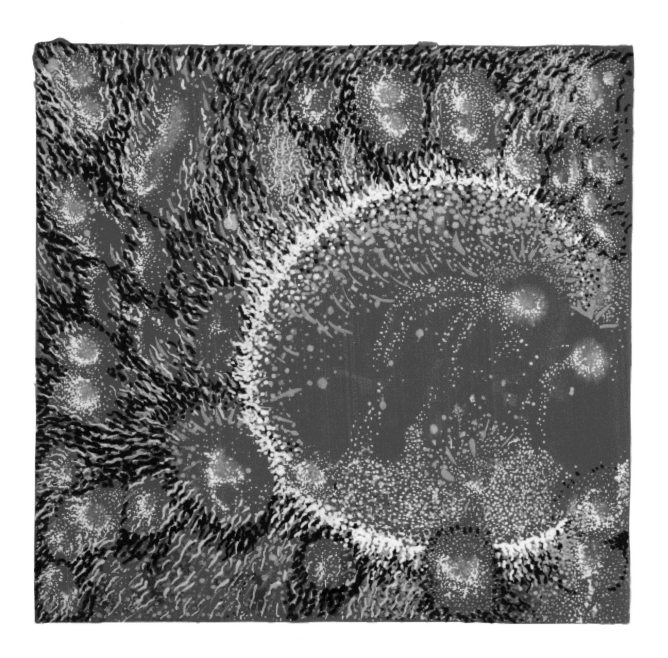

Keys Of Light

Light Forming

Inner Light

Illumination

Kindness

By observing the subtle forms of light, the wonder of change is revealed. Light has many mysterious properties. Light makes more light, and light makes 'light of things'. There is also the creation of light from within. You illuminate this world, and the dark. The spontaneous action and natural expression of light creates kindness. This is the inner light which is free to go in any direction without restrictions. Deep within yourself there are no restrictions.

Light Forming

Boundless energy

Here is an aerial view from above the clouds. High up here, in the silence, while trying to look at the Earth below, your attention is caught by energy that is electrifying, connecting, and expanding. Light is forming, but it's already light, diffusing, dispersing, making more light. This is the creation of subtle, almost musical, influences. It's a clear sky, and a beautiful day. It's spring. New beginnings.

Here is a source of boundless energy that you can tap into. In this turquoise you can take-in as much energy as you need. Become aware of the energy of the day, as the light filters down and infuses everything. Even as you walk through it, you receive it.

Expansive   Refreshing   Magical

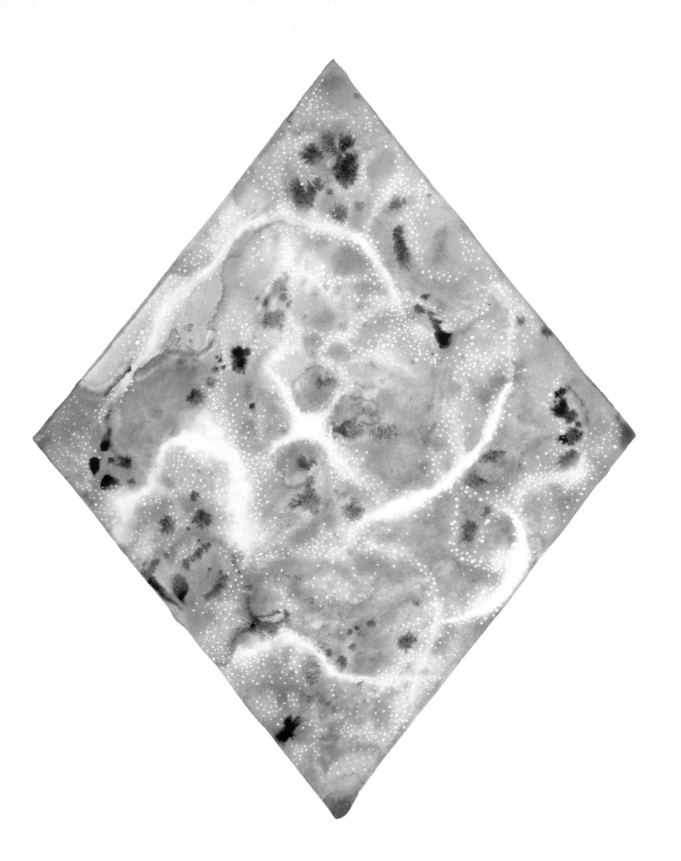

Inner Light

Opening the treasure chest

To the anemone the water is like air, in which it moves and breathes, and floats free. The water provides the environment and you can almost hear its' flow. The anemone is rooted in tiny golden pebbles adding individual weight and support. The anemone comes alive, and it lights-up its' environment. The light from the anemone sings-out, like the opening of a treasure chest under water. The golden pearls hidden for so long, and newly discovered, shine-out.

Energy is directed upward to a new element at the apex, where the air is cool, spacious, and very still. The falling white snow energy blends with the light of the anemone. Here in this receptive space the anemone continues to pour out its' own energy. When you are born and live in an environment you change the nature of it by your presence.

Happiness   Flow   Freedom

Illumination

To see beyond

The night sky is touching the Earth. By staying still and adjusting to the night scene, the energies of the Earth can be seen. The energies are very different from the panorama in daylight. At night the energies of Earth come alive, creating another world or element. You have to feel your way through the scene engaging all your senses, taking-in everything on a much closer scale, like tiny drops of dew on a blade of grass. This is where intuition comes into its' own. The obvious is removed, leaving only the subtle, which is revealed through senses other than eyesight. Subtle light and shadows can be made out, and the scene repeats itself on different levels. You are invited to move deeper into the night scene. The way is illuminated.

As you move towards the apex it seems to become even quieter. It is perfectly safe. It is the magical night. It is possible to see beyond the physical, and you already feel your way through the world with your senses and intuition. You already exist beyond the physical, in your thoughts and feelings, your insight and intuition. These are part of the intangible worlds. Use your insight to see beyond, and you will find the physical world is illuminated both day and night.

Vision   Intuition   Mysterious

Kindness

Natural expression

From deep within, energy is rising, causing positive change. Light emerges through the darker slow-moving energy, pouring-out and bubbling-up to the surface. There are extremes of temperature, of cool and heat. It is the meeting of two extremes that causes change. Nothing is stable. Although powerful, all this movement takes place gently at its' own pace. There is room for all of this to happen. There is freedom of movement without control.

An expression without thought directly from deep within the heart follows the path of least resistance. Light breaks through the darkest areas, regardless of the conditions. The spiritual is expressed in any conditions. Kindness is a spontaneous expression of light, without the need for recognition, or gratitude. This is an expression of positive change for no reason at all.

Spontaneous   Consideration   Giving

Keys Of Freedom

The Crescent Array

The Present Moment

The Rainbow Golden Dawn

The intangible touches Earth. Spiritual energy permeates stillness, and everything physical changes. Being open to new positive influences brings-in change. You create stability in your own heart, and optimism in the present moment. Through awareness you have a place in the infinite.

The Crescent Array

A Light Identity

In the day the trees and grasses reach-out into the light and air, and at night the darkness and energy of the universe reaches down through them into the Earth. At night you can actually see the starry heavens touch the edge of every tree and blade of grass. The night sky although quiet, speaks, and the Earth receives.

At night, and less obviously during the day, there is a relaxation of all activity, and this makes it possible for you to listen and take-in energy. The process of giving and receiving, of breathing-in and breathing-out, is the natural flow of the universe. When this receptive flow of energy is in balance 'The Reflective Protecting Light' comes into being as a perfect blending of the energies. During the day stillness can be seen in the pure reflective white light. At night the radiant array of the night sky touches Earth and the depths of the universe can be felt. Spiritual energy is being received by, and through, the Earth.

Two crescents form part of this world. The blue starry heavens, and the orange-terracotta and green leopard camouflage pattern of Earth. The golden light from the North Pole reaches down, forming a strong reflective filigree veil of protection. As it filters out into the night sky the filigree dissipates into the stars. This is the point of reception of the unknown.

We all want to blend with the Earth, to be protected, but at the same time, we want to be independent. To be spiritually independent we need to be 'light' enough to take-on the unknown. We have the capacity to 'shine-out'. This process of forming a 'Light Identity' culminates in a spontaneous expression of vitality, enthusiasm, and humour. A light identity illuminates naturally.

Polarity   Reflection   Reception

The Present Moment

Acknowledging the Infinite

Orange and yellow dominate, creating warmth and comfort like a sandy substance. This is the assurance of familiarity, place, and family, and the acknowledgment of time and human history. You expand your influence over this soft sandy effect of the yellows and oranges, that have spread across a sea of indigo.

Beyond the soft orange, light energy is moving out, or spinning, at speed, creating the reflective shield of certainty and potential in the present moment. This reflective spinning is fast, creating space, and the refreshing energy of optimism. The indigo has been reduced to a crescent, demarcated and acknowledged by a line of turquoise blue.

The indigo crescent is that which is beyond thought, nothing, and unknown. The uncertainty is covered-over. Its' opposite, in the orange crescent, is the joy and expression of being alive in the present moment. This crescent is tipped with bright red, which makes contact with the indigo. Everything physical in life, in the red, touches the edge of nothing, in the indigo. Here the red and indigo hold hands in perfect balance, as if 'taking the bull by the horns'.

This is a perspective on the transient nature of life, as a process beyond control or explanation. This leads to an appreciation of the turn of events, whether right or wrong, satisfying or unjust, and also an acceptance of the present. Here is a blend of the action and uncertainty in life, and being comfortable in your own heart. There is a feeling of time and timelessness, of speed and calm. An acceptance that, in the vastness of uncertainty, you are here now, creating a permanence in the present moment.

Permanence   Unknown   Strength

Rainbow Golden Dawn

A new beginning

When you see the wonder, on any day, when you are still and clear, you reflect 'wonder'. As in a spyglass, or seeing it reflected on its' lens, afar off, yet seen close. Within the sphere of clarity there is a quiet, unassuming, quality that slowly changes with the golden dawn reflection. This is the landscape of being aware. Beauty, wonder, and great depth, are transformed by the dawn, as you are by awareness. New life is introduced as the pinks turn the blues to violets, and the yellows turn the pinks to orange. The golden dawn is an influence giving confidence, assurance, and insight. Everything is becoming, blossoming, deepening. You are constantly beginning. Ideas, ideals, and views change. Relationships change. You are not the same person you thought you were yesterday. This is a new spiritual dawn. Through your awareness you have a place in the infinite. Welcome to the wonder.

Influence   Clearness   Reflect

The Keys Of Awareness   Page Numbers

43
Shining Out

57
Light Energy

63
Wonder

75
Forgiveness

95
Behind The Veil

97
The Guiding Star

115
Inner Light

117
Illumination

35
The Tapestry of Life

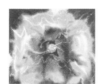

49
Lion Heart

59
Expansion

65
Soundless Space

73
Living in the Clouds

79
Lotus Light

89
The Theatre of Life

109
The Unbroken Stone

47
Touching Earth

55
Angel

83
The Buddha's Temple

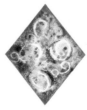

99
Cornucopia

The Keys Of Awareness　　Page Numbers

39
The Garden

33
Creation

53
Beautiful World

69
The Prayer Wheel

77
Pearl

87
The Untarnished Shield

103
Constellations

105
The Seasons

123
The Crescent Array

125
The Present Moment

127
Rainbow Golden Dawn

37
Pillar of Flame

45
Incandescence

67
Testament

85
The Winged Dragon

107
Everlasting Flame

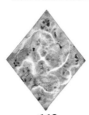

113
Light Forming

93
Contact

119
Kindness

Rachael Wilmot has 15 years experience running classes and groups on meditation, psychic development, Reiki, in-depth courses on colour, and teaching people how to see, and paint, the Energies. Rachael originally trained as a musician at Huddersfield School of Music, followed by a 3 year Combined Degree in Music and Fine Art at Brighton. She started with figurative painting based on spiritual insights, but in the past 10 years has moved on to painting the Energies directly. Rachael paints the energies she sees. These are the intangible living energies that surround and support everything, and come through in our awareness and well-being.

If you would like to choose and work with a particular Key
for contemplation and meditation, each Key is available
in its' original shape separately, in a larger size
(25 X 35 cm. approx overall dimensions) printed on thick card.
See web site for full details.

illustriousartworks.com